HAWAII
VISITING A VOLCANO

by Anne Franklin

SCHOOL PUBLISHERS

Cover, ©Jim Sugar/Science Faction/Getty Images; p.3, ©PhotoDisc Red/Punch Stock; p.5, p.6, p.12, ©Bigbamboostock.com; p.7, (l) ©Bigbamboostock.com, (r) ©Douglas Peebles/CORBIS; p.8, (tl) ©Michael Ord/Photo Researchers, Inc., (r) ©Douglas Peebles Photography/Alamy; p.9, ©Douglas Peebles Photography/Alamy; p.10, ©Roger Ressmeyer/Photographer's Choice/Getty Images; p.11, ©Robert Reiff/Taxi/Getty Images; p.13, ©Andre Jenny/Alamy; p.14, ©Donna and Steve O'Meara/Super Stock.

Cartography, p.4, Joe LeMonnier

Printed in China

ISBN 10: 0-15-350534-6
ISBN 13: 978-0-15-350534-8

Ordering Options
ISBN 10: 0-15-350334-3 (Grade 4 Below-Level Collection)
ISBN 13: 978-0-15-350334-4 (Grade 4 Below-Level Collection)
ISBN 10: 0-15-357529-8 (package of 5)
ISBN 13: 978-0-15-357529-7 (package of 5)

5 6 7 8 9 10   985   12 11 10 09

From a distant place on the island of Hawaii, a visitor sees red sparks in the sky. The sparks shoot up from the top of a mountain. This mountain is a volcano called Kilauea [kē' lou ā' ə].

Long ago, there were no islands in the Pacific Ocean where Hawaii is today. It took millions of years for volcanoes to form the islands of Hawaii. A volcano is a large mountain that is formed from hot, melted rock called lava. The melted rock shoots out of the Earth. Over millions of years the lava builds up, forming a large mountain.

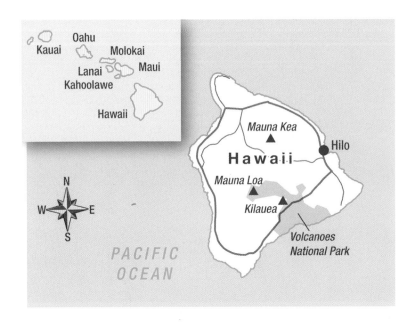

The volcano at Kilauea is one of the world's most active. It is in Volcanoes National Park in the state of Hawaii on the island of Hawaii.

To travel through Volcanoes National Park, you must first make sure you will be safe. Visitors wear heavy boots. They carry binoculars to watch the lava from far away. Visitors make sure they have lots of water, too. It can get very hot close to the volcanoes.

You begin your trip at the Visitor Center. You learn where it is safe to go and where there might be danger. Every day the park changes. That is because the volcanoes in the park can erupt at any time. Lava can flow anywhere, too.

The best way to see Kilauea is to drive around Crater Rim Drive. The top of the volcano has a large hole, or crater. The trip around Crater Rim Drive is 11 miles (17.7 km) long.

Your drive takes you through an ancient rain forest. Here, you see a bird called a nene [nā′ nā′] flutter across the sky. This bird is the Hawaiian goose, the state bird of Hawaii. Nenes fly in large groups called flocks. The nene has a blue band around its leg. A park worker put the band there when the bird was little. The bands help workers keep track of the birds. They learn more about where the birds go to nest and have their young.

As you look out over the land, you wonder, "How did all of these plants get onto this island?" Everywhere, there are flowers in all colors of the rainbow. The land is filled with flowering greens, blues, yellows, and pinks. It was not always that way. Over hundreds of years, wind and water carried seeds from miles away. The plants grew in the dust and ash formed from the erupting volcanoes. They grew into very beautiful plants, some of which cannot be found anywhere else in the world.

Liwi

Palila

Now you see a brightly colored bird with a red head and bill. This is the liwi, a native bird of Hawaii. *Native* means it is a bird that has always lived here. Another bird, the yellow palila, sings in the bushes. "How did the birds get to the islands?" you think. Some may have come on floating logs. Others may have had eggs that floated for many, many miles to get here. Like the plants on the island, many birds here are not found anywhere else in the world.

The different birds on the island have different shaped bills. The long curved bill of the liwi fits deep into narrow flowers. This allows the bird to feed on the tasty nectar of the flower. In contrast, the bill of the palila is curved and short. This bird feeds by cracking seeds open with its powerful bill. The island birds feed on different kinds of flowers and seeds. Many birds are able to live together in the islands because they eat different kinds of foods.

The sun is high in the sky. The rocks in the lava fields glisten in the sun. Through your binoculars, you can see a large cloud of steam rising in the sky far away where the lava meets the ocean. Waves cascading onto the hot lava cause the steam to rise. Signs warn visitors not to go near the beach. Hot lava flows into the water. Sometimes the water gets hot enough to burn people if they are not careful.

Now you see flowing lava far away. Large clouds of gas rise in the air. Lava causes these gases. The gases can hurt people. Visitors are warned not to breathe in the gases. You are glad you are far away. Workers stand like sentries around places you are not allowed to go. They warn visitors of the dangers of the hot lava and gases.

Next you come upon a large field with strange pictures embedded in the rock. The pictures in the rocks are petroglyphs. They are the art of the early Hawaiian people. They are pictures that are carved into the hard lava near the ocean.

The pictures are of straight lines and half circles. There are pictures of circles with dots in the center. Some pictures even look like stick figures of people. As you walk among the stone pictures, you wonder what they mean.

People who journeyed around the island long ago made many of the pictures. You see a picture of a crooked line. Your guidebook tells you that it is a picture of a lizard. Some of the dots and circles are meant to show people, too. People must stay on a wooden path away from the stone pictures to help prevent the stone pictures from eroding over time.

The sun is getting low in the sky now. It has been a long day out on the volcano. You begin to feel weary.

The sun sets over Kilauea. From far away, you can see the glowing red lava of the volcano. Kilauea has had lava flows nearly every day for almost twenty years. The sights and sounds of the rain forest contrast sharply with the open spaces of the lava fields. You are one of the lucky visitors to see red lava flowing up close. At night, you close your eyes and remember the brightly colored lava lighting up the sky.

Think Critically

1. Why must people be careful when visiting the volcano park?

2. What are some sights a person might see while driving along Crater Rim Drive?

3. What causes steam to rise from the ocean waters at the base of the volcano?

4. Why do you think that the volcanoes on Hawaii have been made into a national park?

5. Would you like to see Kilauea volcano? Explain why or why not.

Science

Draw a Diagram Find out about the parts of an active volcano. Then draw a diagram of the volcano. Label the parts of the volcano on your diagram.

 School-Home Connection Find out about a rain forest animal that you like. Draw a picture of the animal, how it lives, and what it eats. Share what you learned with a friend or family member.

Word Count: 1,011 (1,013)